Willow the Witch Celebrates Samhain

LUCY CRANN

Copyright © 2023 Kaitlyn Finn

All rights reserved.

ISBN: 9798322660651

DEDICATION

To my Ancestors.

ACKNOWLEDGMENTS

This story was illustrated with the assistance of AI (with a lot of human intervention)

In a world where Autumn's chill whispers secrets old,
Lives Willow the Witch brave and bold.

With Frog the Cat, whose eyes are a mysterious hue,
They awaited Samhain, under a sky of blue.

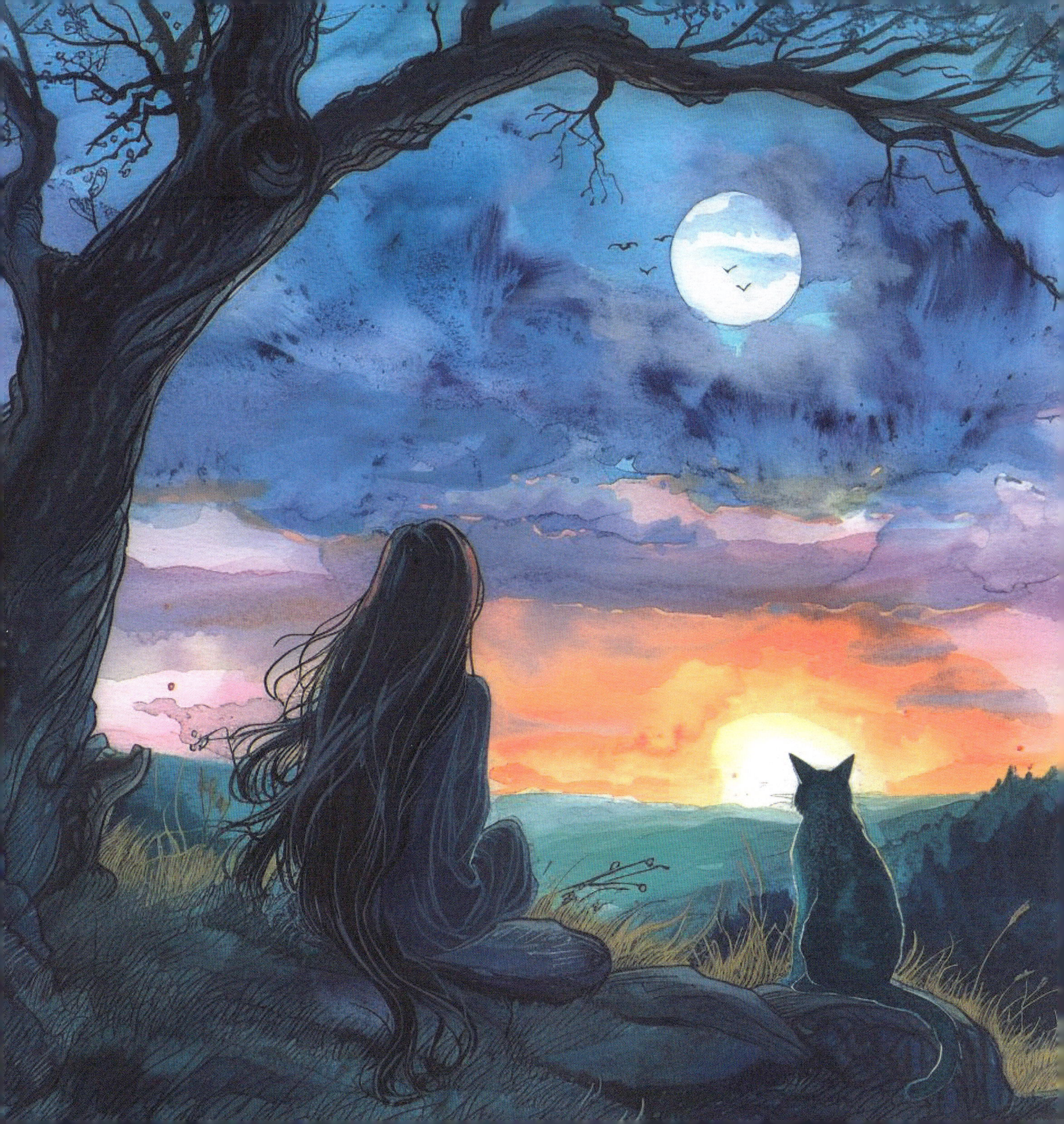

"Samhain's veil is thinning," Willow spoke with a smile,
"Let's honor the ancestors in a way that's worthwhile.

With Candles and stories, and photos so dear,
We'll invite them to join us and feel them near."

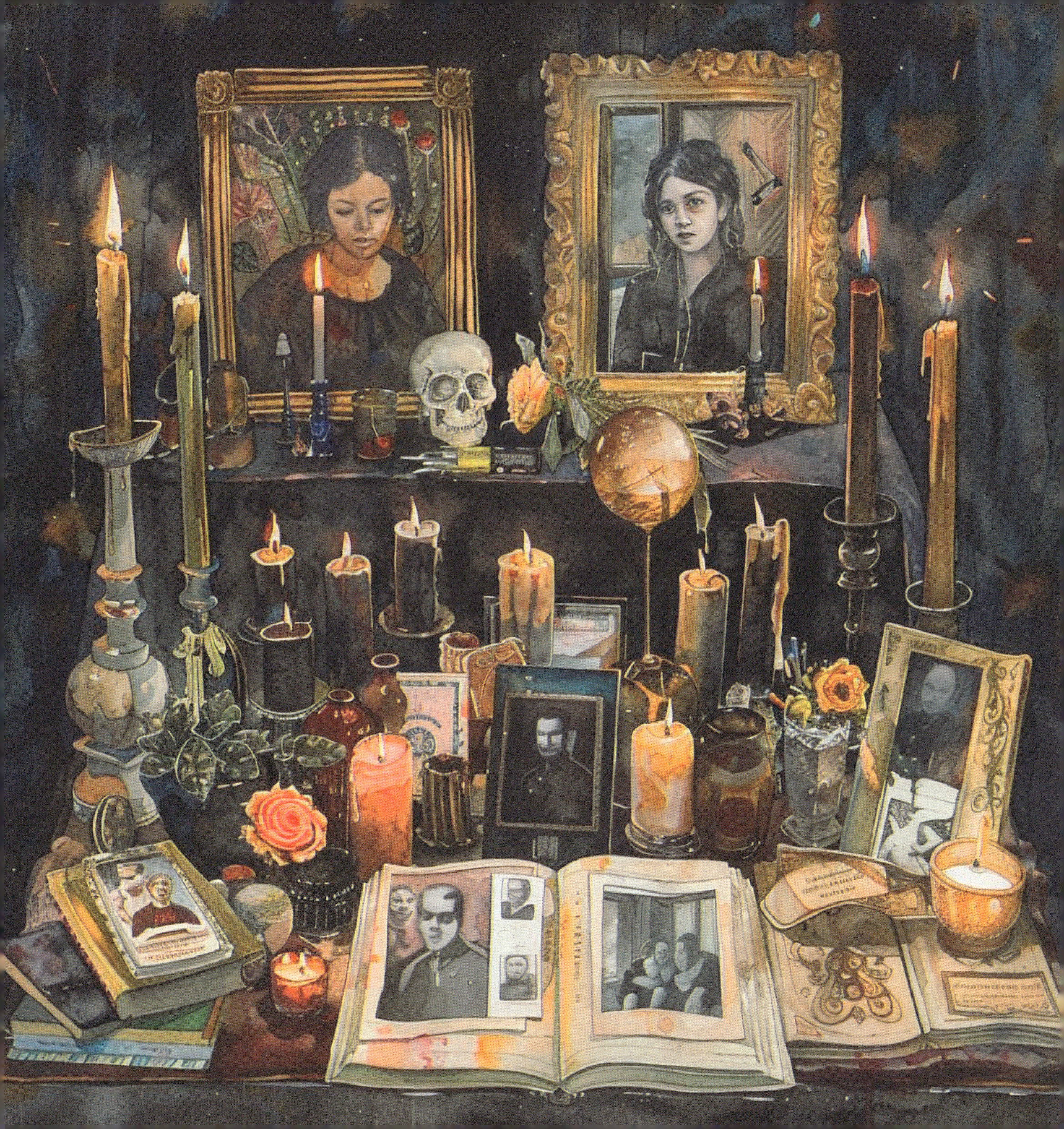

They set to work in the garden, under the Moon's soft glow,
Planting pumpkins and gourds and watching them grow.

"Carve them with faces both spooky and sweet,"
Willow laughed as Frog the Cat danced at her feet.

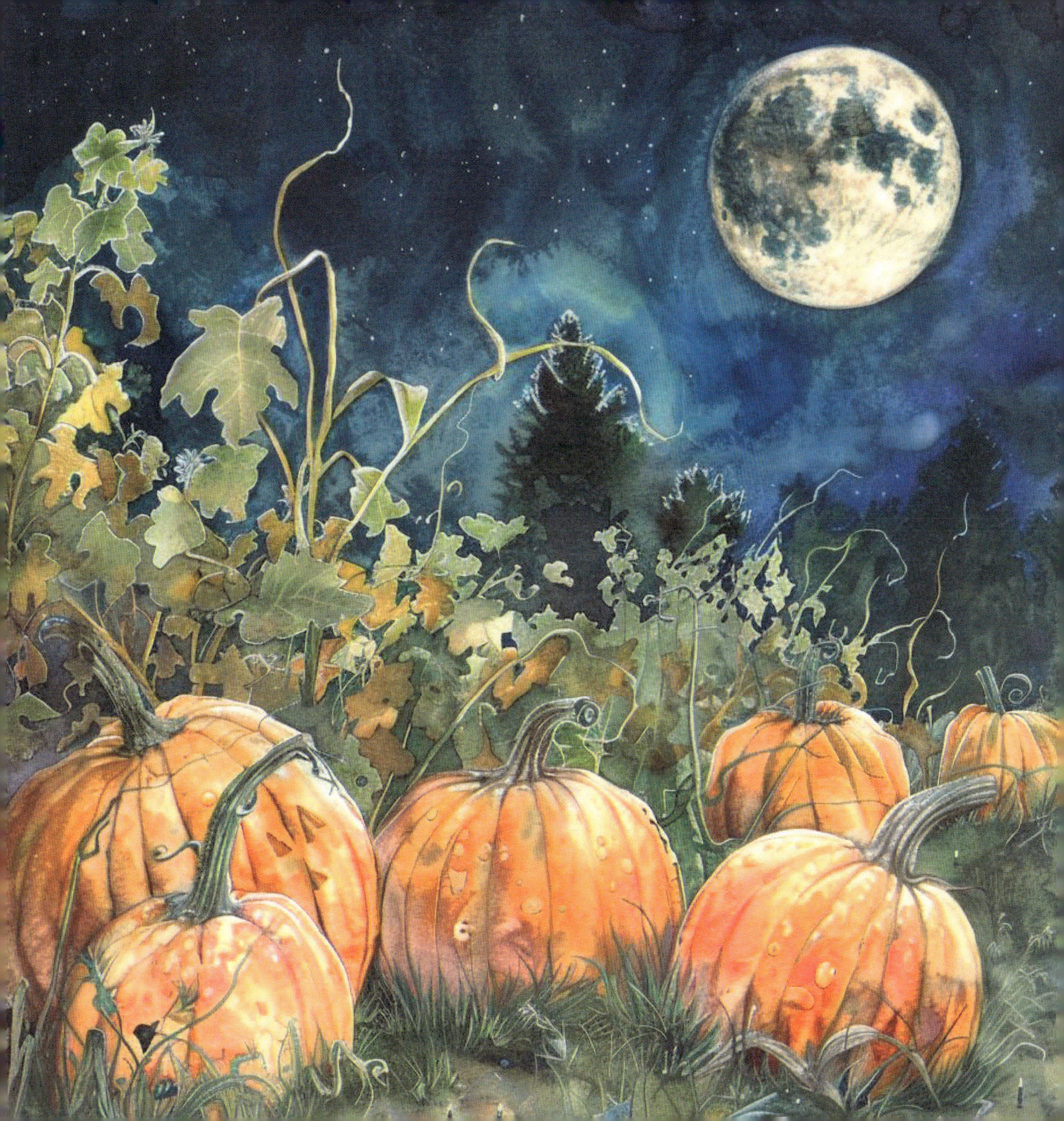

Inside their cozy cottage, they prepared a feast,
With Autumn's bounty, from greatest to least.

"Apples for wisdom, pomegranates for the dead,
Let's lay out a plate for the spirits." Willow said.

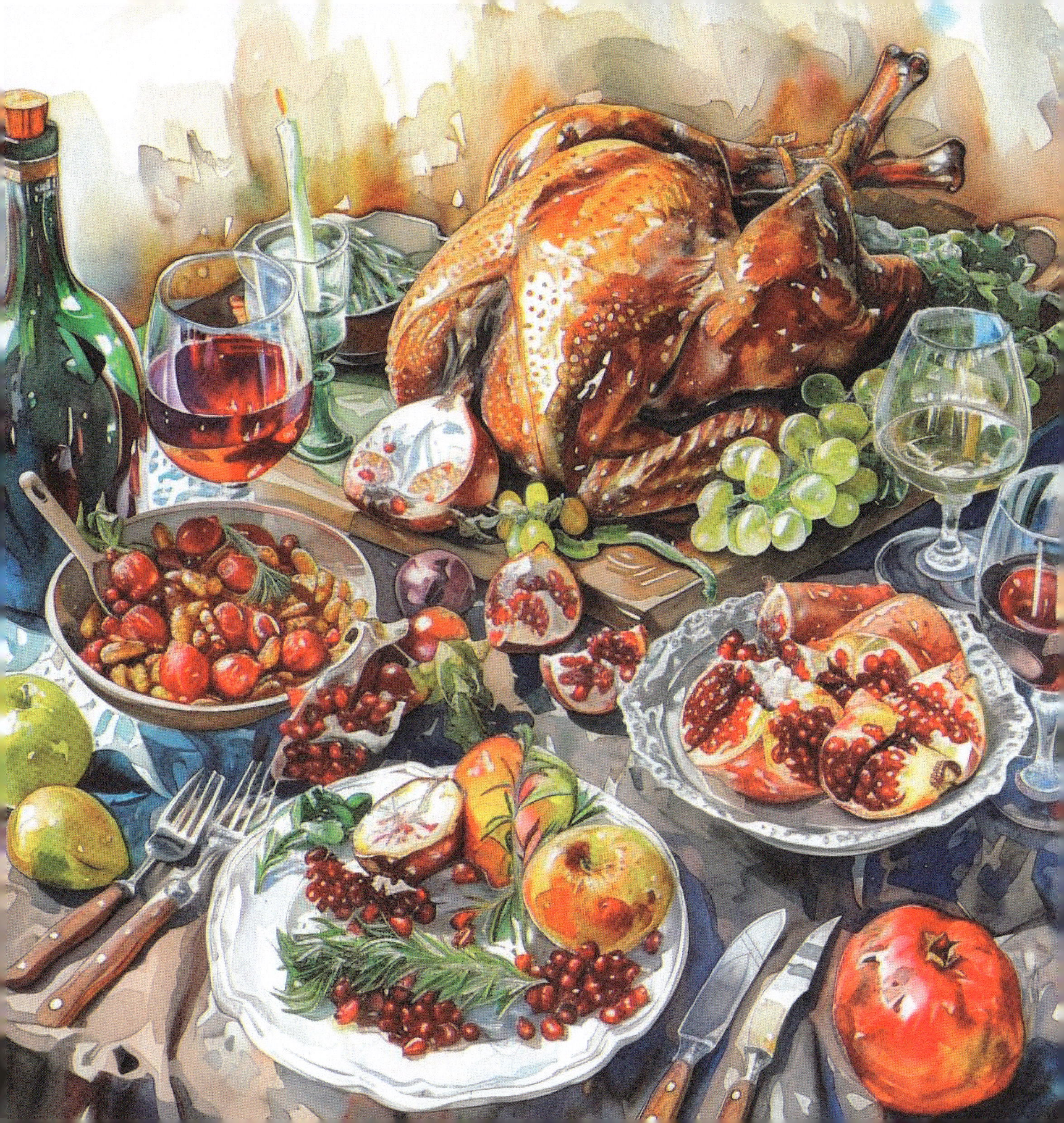

Willow cast a big circle, with branches bare from the cold,
A sacred space, where magic tales could be told.

"Frog my dear bring the lanterns, let's light them up bright.
To guide the spirits home, on this Samhain night."

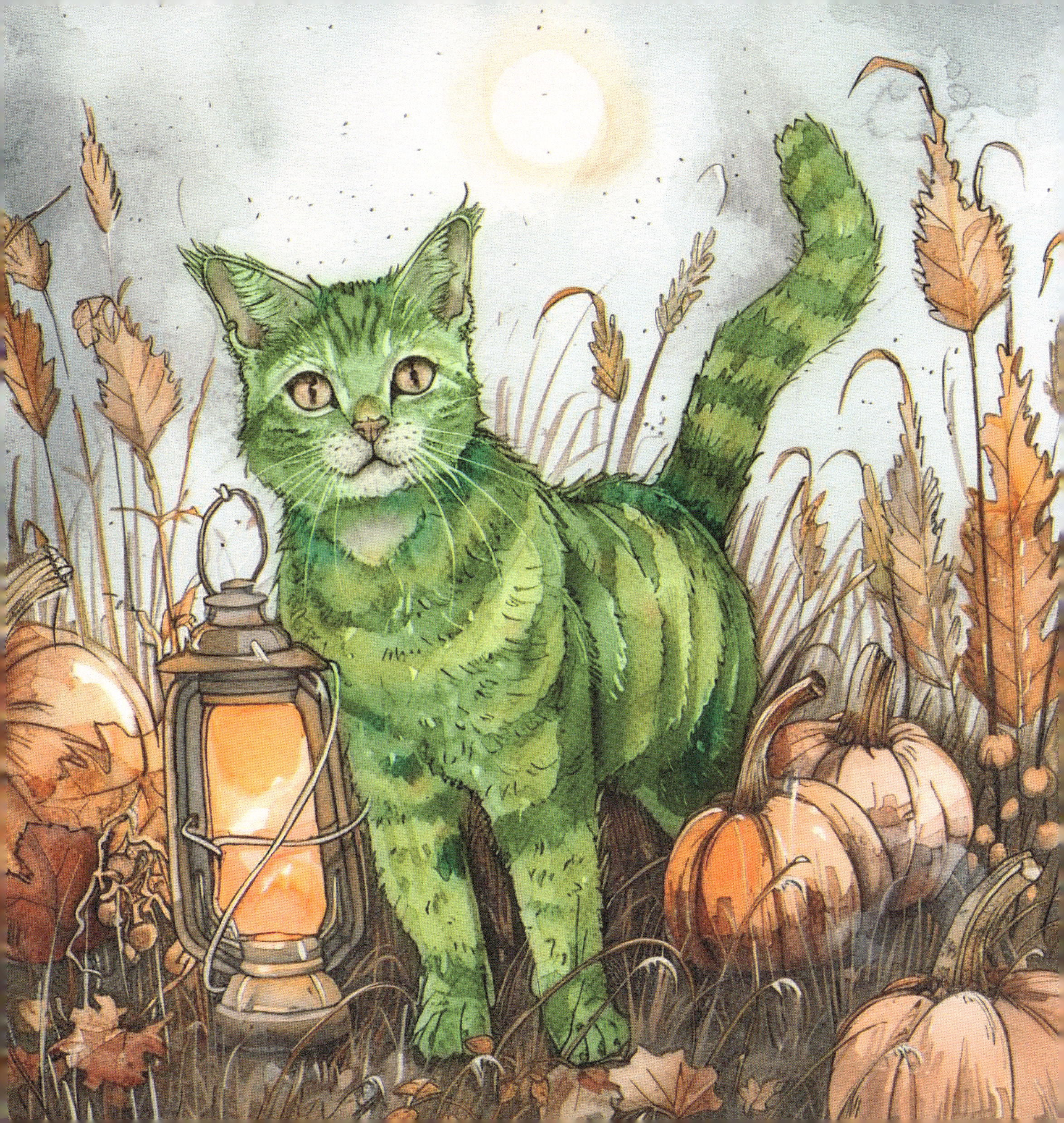

Willow dressed in a cloak of the deepest black,
With Frog the Cat following along her track.

Together they whispered some ancient spells,
Invoking protection with her witch's bells.

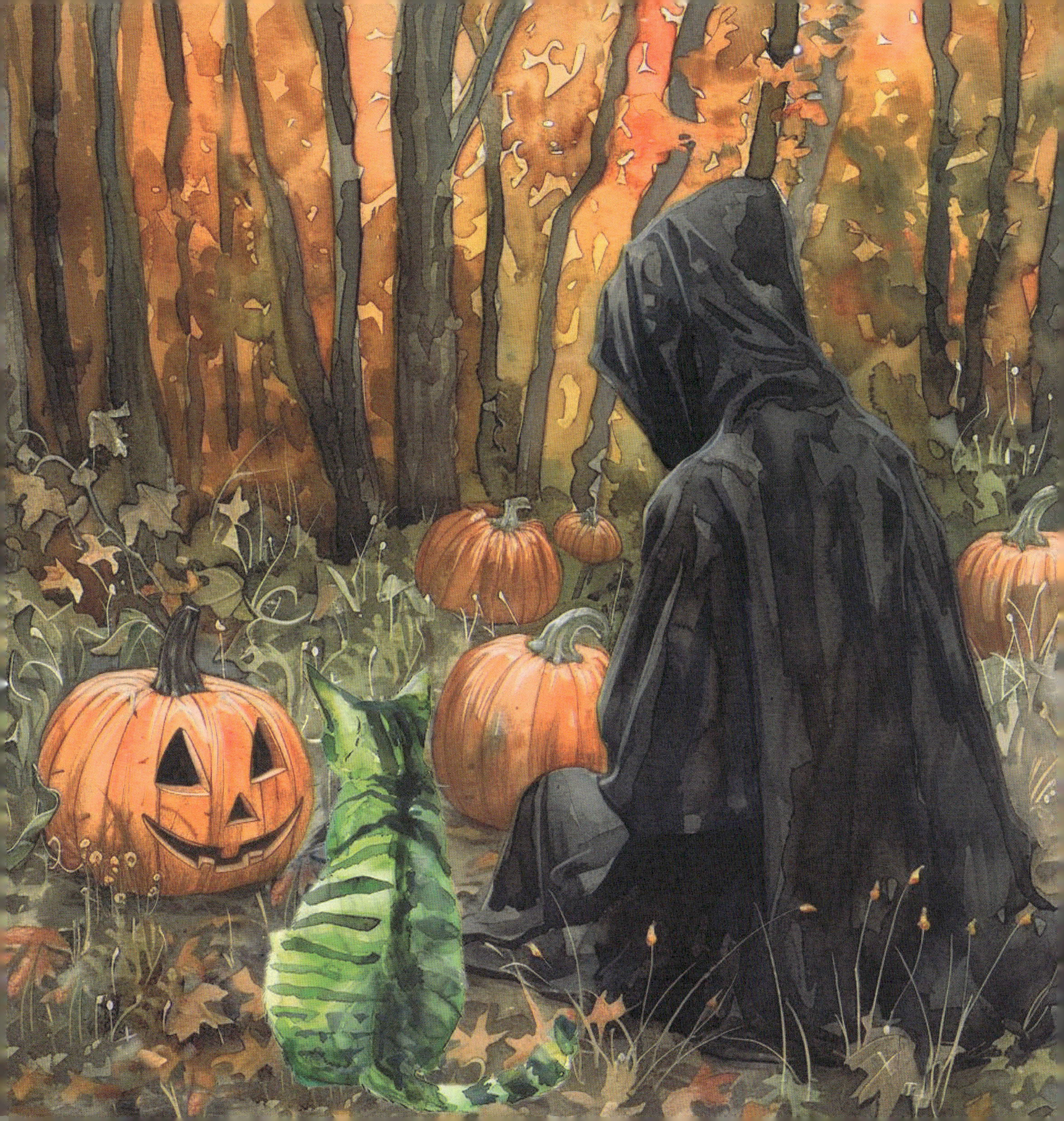

"Let's remember those who walked before,"
Willow said as she opened the Spirit's door.

They shared memories, both sweet and sour,
Feeling the Ancestor's calm guiding power.

As midnight approached, the air grew still.
Willow and Frog felt a loving chill.

"Spirits of the past, hear our call!
Join us in peace, one and all."

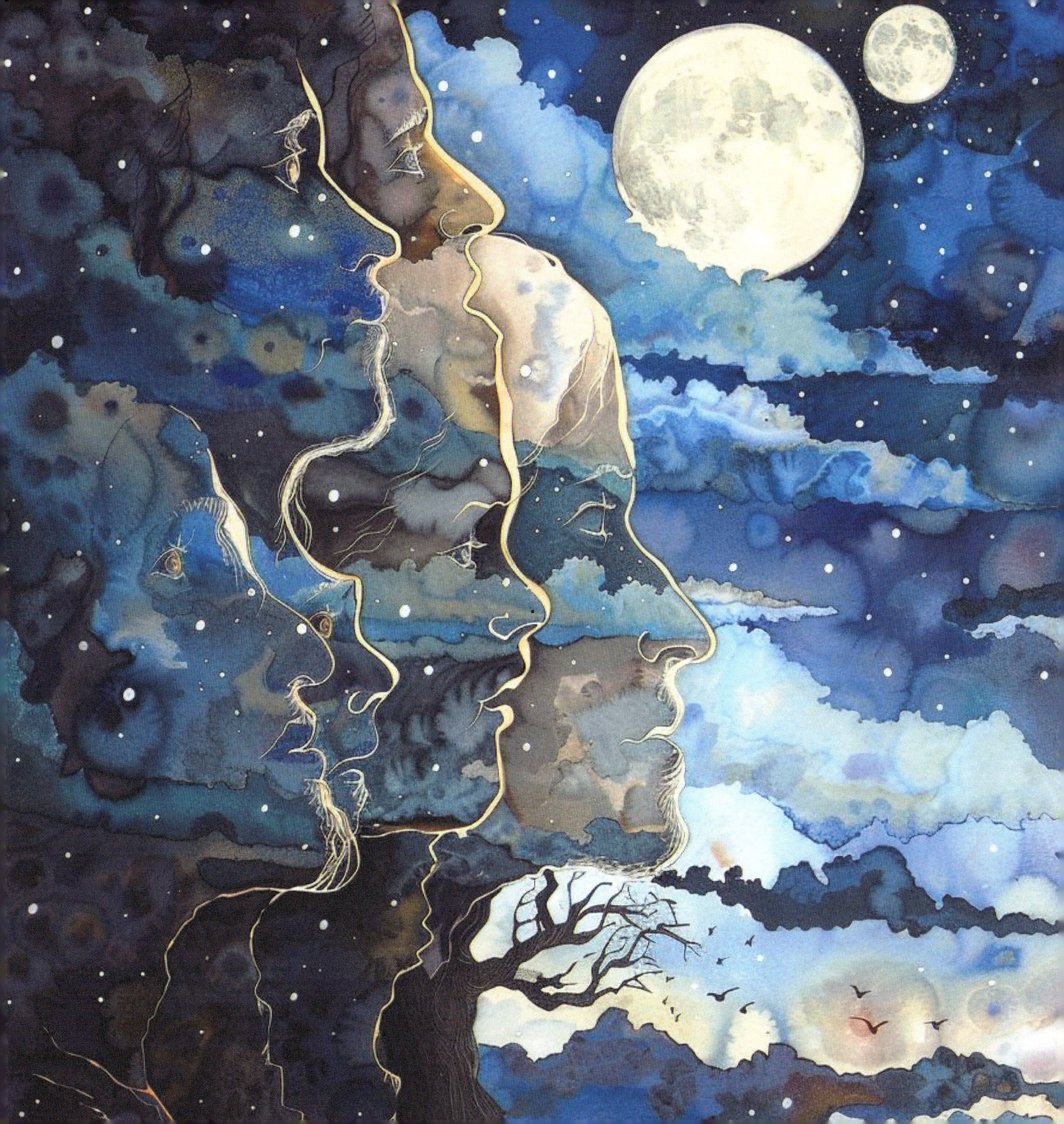

They danced by the fire, with shadows grown long,
Chanting and laughing, a heartfelt song.

The spirits whispered in the rustling leaves,
Blessings received as the spells veil weaved.

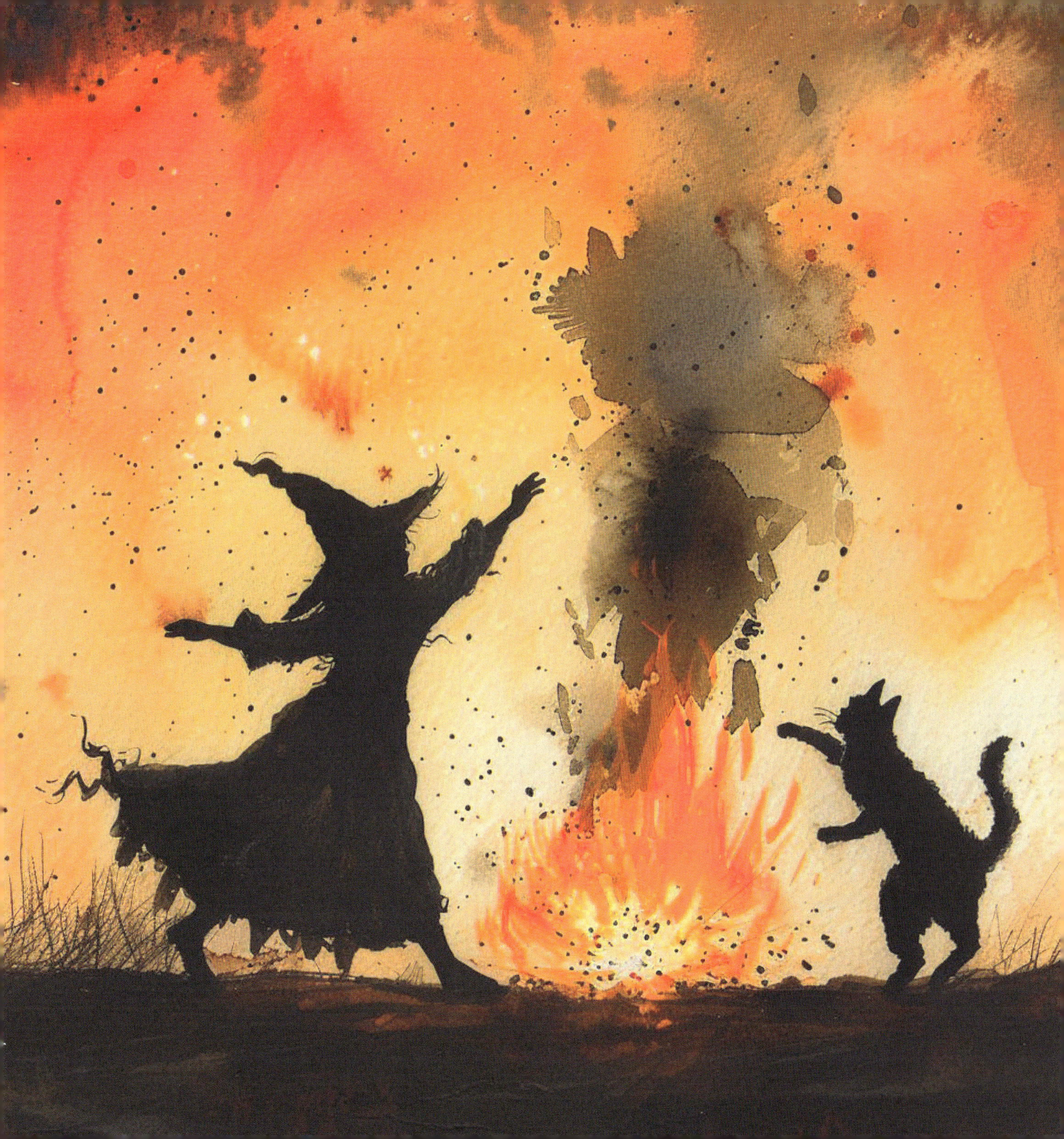

With the first light of dawn, the air crisp and clear,
Willow and Frog sensed the ancient spirits were near.

"Thankyou," they whispered, "for your presence last night,"
Who were feeling enriched by the ancestral sight.

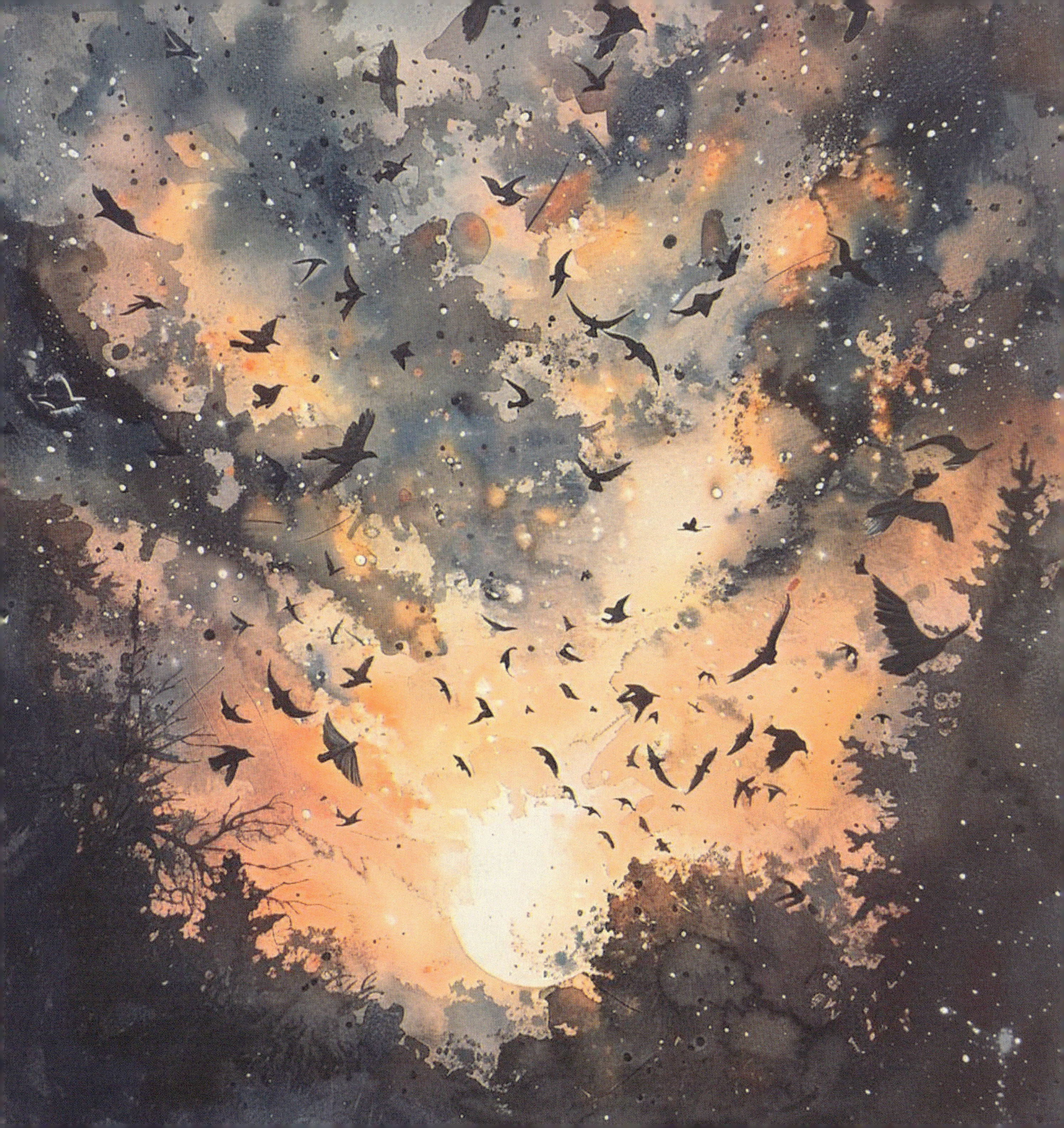

As Samhain night closed, and the world awoke,
Willow and Frog slept on beneath an ancient oak.

They felt the cycle of life, and the wisdom it spoke,
In the magic of Samhain and of the Fae Folk.

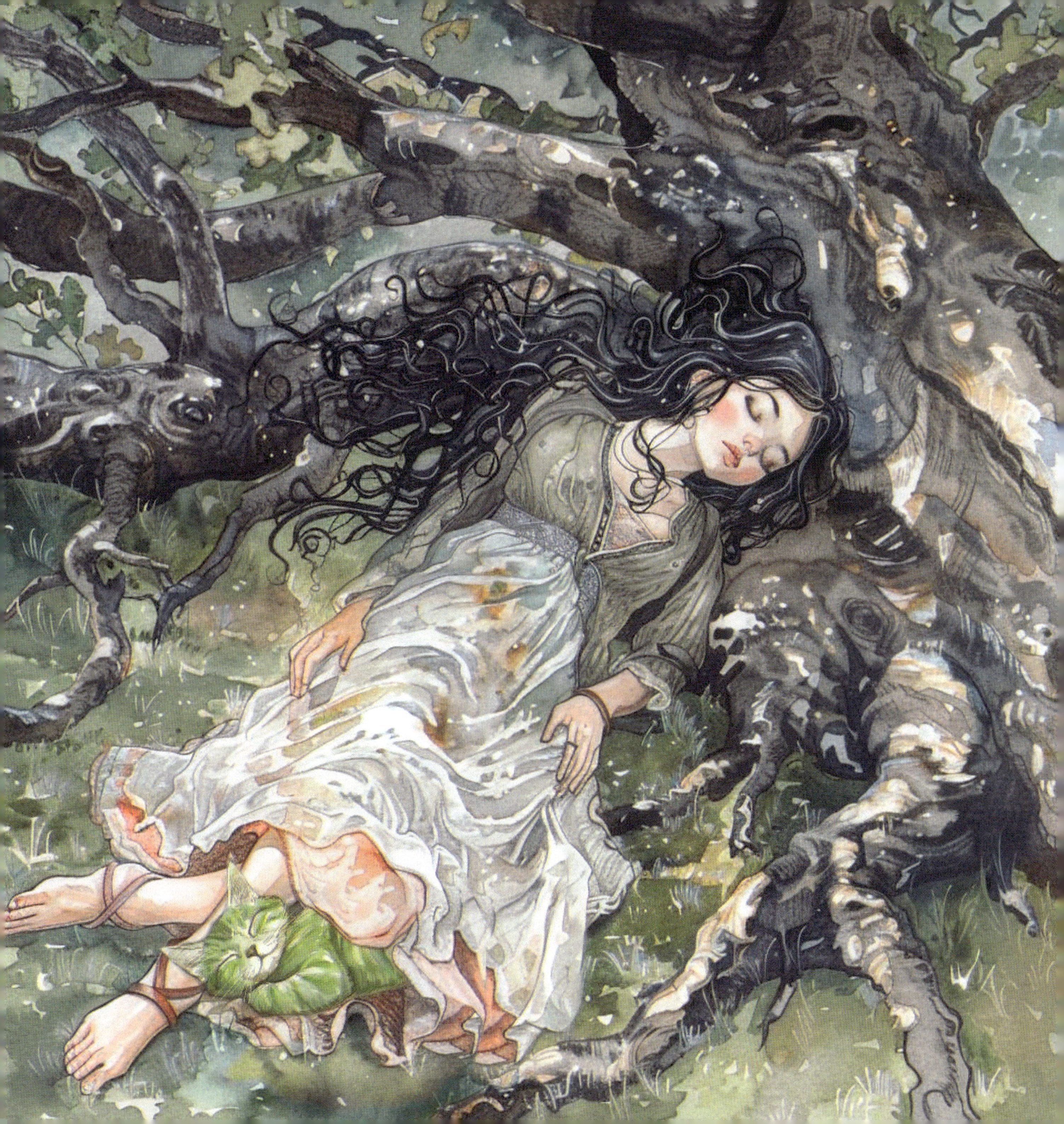

So let this tale of shadows and of light,
Guide you gently through the night.

With Willow and Frog, we embrace what may come,
For in the Wheel of the Year, we are all united as one.

ABOUT THE AUTHOR

Lucy Crann is an Australian author striving to fill the void of books for young pagans and witches alike.

Printed in Great Britain
by Amazon